It's a Caterpillar!

¡Es una oruga!

Elisa Peters

Traducción al español:
Eduardo Alamán

PowerKiDS press™ & **Editorial Buenas Letras**™

New York

For Brodie Patrick Sullivan

Published in 2009 by The Rosen Publishing Group, Inc.
29 East 21st Street, New York, NY 10010

First Edition

Editor: Amelie von Zumbusch
Book Design: Greg Tucker
Photo Researcher: Jessica Gerweck

Photo Credits: All Images by Shutterstock.com.

Library of Congress Cataloging-in-Publication Data

Peters, Elisa.
  [It's a caterpillar! Spanish & English]
  It's a caterpillar! = ¡Es una oruga! / Elisa Peters ; traducción al español, Eduardo Alamán. – 1st ed.
       p. cm. – (Everyday wonders = Maravillas de todos los días)
  Added t.p. title: ¡Es una oruga!
  Includes index.
  ISBN 978-1-4358-2524-6 (library binding)
  1. Caterpillars–Juvenile literature. I. Title. II. Title: ¡Es una oruga!
  QL544.2.P4818 2009
  595.78'139–dc22
                                                2008003886

Manufactured in the United States of America

Web Sites: Due to the changing nature of Internet links, PowerKids Press and Editorial Buenas Letras have developed an online list of Web sites related to the subject of this book. This site is updated regularly. Please use this link to access the list:
www.powerkidslinks.com/wonder/caterpillar/

Contents/Contenido

This bug is a caterpillar.

Este insecto es una oruga.

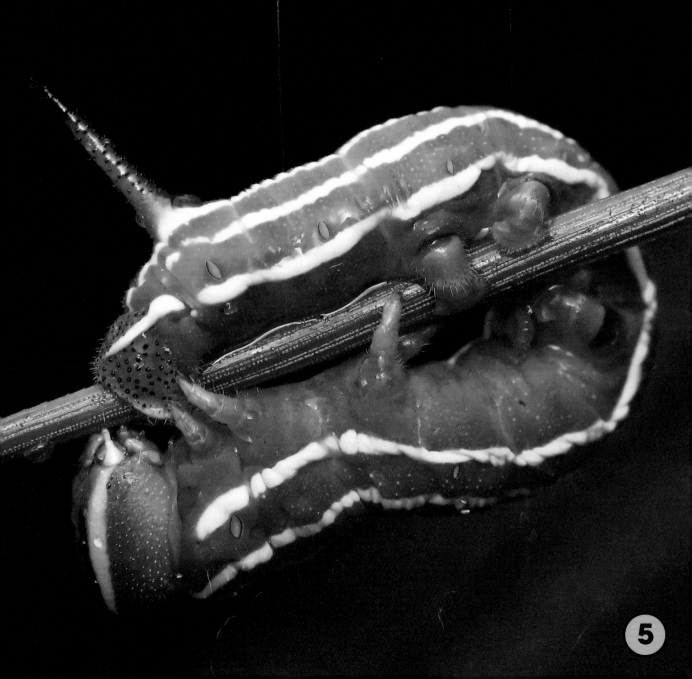

Caterpillars have a long,
soft body.

Las orugas tienen un cuerpo
largo y suave.

⑦

Caterpillars come in many different colors.

Las orugas pueden ser de muchos colores distintos.

Some caterpillars have **stripes**.

Algunas orugas tienen **rayas**.

⑪

Other caterpillars are **hairy**.

Otras orugas son **peludas**.

There are even caterpillars
with **spikes**!

¡Algunas orugas
tienen **púas**!

When caterpillars are in danger, they roll up in a ball.

Cuando las orugas están en peligro se arrollan formando una bola.

Caterpillars eat leaves. They eat a lot.

Las orugas comen
las hojas de los árboles.
Las orugas comen mucho.

In time, a caterpillar becomes a **pupa**.

Con el tiempo, las orugas se convierten en **crisálidas**.

21

Finally, the pupa turns into a moth or a butterfly!

Finalmente, la crisálida se convierte en una polilla o en una mariposa.

Words to Know/Palabras que debes saber

hairy/peluda

pupa
(la) crisálida

spikes
(las) púas

stripes
(las) rayas

Index

Índice